PANDA WHITE
AND THE SEVEN
SMALL ANIMALS

TEXT AND ILLUSTRATIONS BY TERRY WALTZ

A PandaRiffic! Book for Early Chinese as a Second Language Readers

Squid For Brains
Albany, NY

Panda White and the Seven Small Animals
(Simplified Character Version)
Terry T. Waltz

Published by Squid For Brains
Albany, NY

ISBN-13: 978-0692730690
ISBN-10: 0692730699

从前 有 一只 河马。 这只 河马 很
漂亮。 她 比 美国小姐 漂亮。 她 比 JLo
漂亮。 她 比 Bustin Jeeber 漂亮。 没有 人
比 她 漂亮。

河马 说:「我 很 漂亮!」
(河马 漂亮 不 漂亮? 不 漂亮!)

Cóngqián yǒu yìzhī hémǎ. zhèzhī hémǎ hěn piàoliang. Tā bǐ měiguó xiǎojiě piàoliang. Tā bǐ JLo piàoliang. tā bǐ Bustin Jeeber piàoliang. Méiyǒu rén bǐ tā piàoliang. Hémǎ shuō: "Wǒ hěn piàoliang!"

(Hémǎ piàoliang bú piàoliang? Bú piàoliang!)

cónGqiáN yǒu YìZHĪ hÉmǎ. ZhèZHĪ hÉmǎ hěn Piàoliang*. TĀ bǐ měiguÓ xiǎojiě Piàoliang*. TĀ bǐ JLo Piàoliang*. TĀ bǐ Bustin Jeeber Piàoliang*. méIyǒu réN bǐ TĀ Piàoliang*. hÉmǎ SHUŌ: "wǒ hěn Piàoliang*!"

(hÉmǎ Piàoliang* Bú Piàoliang*? Bú Piàoliang*!)

　　虽然 河马 不 漂亮， 可是 因为 她 是
女王， 所以 大家 都 跟她 说， 她 很
漂亮。 女王 去 J-Mart 的时候， 她 跟
在 J-Mart 的 人 说： 「你 看 我 漂亮 吗？」
　　在 J-Mart 的 人 都 跟 女王 说： 「很 漂
亮！ 很 漂亮！」

Suīrán hémǎ bú piàoliang, kěshì yīnwèi tā shì nǚwáng, suǒyǐ dàjiā dōu gēntā shuō, tā hěn piàoliang. Nǚwáng qù J-Mart de shíhòu, tā gēn zài J-Mart de rén shuō: "Nǐ kàn wǒ piàoliang ma?" Zài J-Mart de rén gēn nǚwáng shuō: "Hěn piàoliang! hěn piàoliang!"

SUĪráN hÉmǎ bÚ Piàoliang*, kěShì YĪNWèi TĀ Shì nǚwánG, suǒyǐ DàJIĀ DŌU GĒNTĀ SHUŌ, TĀ hěn Piàoliang*. nǚwánG Qù J-Mart de*shíHòu, TĀ GĒN Zài J-Mart de*réN SHUŌ: "nǐ Kàn wǒ Piàoliang* ma*?" Zài J-Mart de*réN GĒN nǚwánG SHUŌ: "hěn Piàoliang*! hěn Piàoliang*!"

　　女王 很 高兴，因为 大家 都 跟她说 她
很 漂亮。
　　女王 喜欢 口红。她的 口红 很多。
红色的，粉红色的，她 都 有。女王 很
喜欢 在 J-Mart 买 口红。

Nǔwáng hěn gāoxìng. yīnwèi dàjiā dōu gēntā shuō tā hěn piàoliang.
Nǔwáng xǐhuān kǒuhóng.
tāde kǒuhóng hěnduō. Hóngsède, fěnhóngsède tā dōu yǒu. Nǔwáng hěn xǐhuān zài J-Mart mǎi kǒuhóng.

nǔwánG hěn GĀOXìng, YĪNWèi DàJIĀ DŌU GĒNTĀ SHUŌ TĀ hěn Piàoliang*.

nǔwánG xǐHUĀN kǒuhónG. TĀde* kǒuhónG hěnDUŌ. hónGSède*, fěnhónGSède* TĀ DŌU yǒu.
nǔwánG hěn xǐHUĀN Zài J-Mart mǎi kǒuhónG.

可是 她 不 高兴， 因为 J-Mart 的 口红 不 比 她 有的 口红 漂亮。

所以 女王 上网。 她 上网 买 口红。 她 上网 买的 口红 比 她 在 J-Mart 买的 口红 漂亮。 女王 上了 KouHong.com 买了 很多 口红。

Kěshì tā bù gāoxìng, yīnwèi J-Mart de kǒuhóng bù bǐ tā yǒude kǒuhóng piàoliang. Suǒyǐ nǚwáng shàngwǎng. Tā shàngwǎng mǎi kǒuhóng. Tā shàngwǎng mǎide kǒuhóng bǐ tā zài J-Mart mǎide kǒuhóng piàoliang. Nǚwáng shàngle kouhong.com mǎile hěnduō kǒuhóng.

kěShì TĀ Bù GĀOXìng, YĪNWèi J-Mart de* kǒuhónG Bù bǐ TĀ yǒude* kǒuhónG Piàoliang*. suǒyǐ nǚwánG Shàngwǎng. TĀ Shàngwǎng mǎi kǒuhónG. TĀ Shàngwǎng mǎide* kǒuhónG bǐ TĀ Zài J-Mart mǎi de* kǒuhónG Piàoliang*. nǚwánG Shàngle* kouhong.com mǎile* hěnDUŌ kǒuhónG.

女王 上网 买 口红 的时候， 她 也 都 上网 看看， 她 是 不是 最 漂亮 的。 有一天， 女王 上网 看 SheiZuiPiaoLiangDe.com 的时候， 她 就 不 高兴 了。 她 不 高兴， 因为 SheiZuiPiaoLiangDe.com 说， 她 不是 最 漂亮 的。 SheiZuiPiaoLiangDe.com 说， Panda White 是 最 漂亮 的。

Nǚwáng shàngwǎng mǎi kǒuhóng deshíhòu, tā yě dōu shàngwǎng kànkàn, tā shìbúshì zuì piàoliangde. Yǒuyītiān, nǚwáng shàngwǎng kàn SheiZuiPiaoLiangDe.com deshíhòu, tā jiù bùgāoxìng le. Tā bù gāoxìng, yīnwèi tāmen shuō, tā búshì zuì piàoliangde. Tāmen shuō, Panda White shì zuì piàoliangde.

nǚwánG Shàngwǎng mǎi kǒuhónG de*shÍHòu, TĀ yě DŌU Shàngwǎng KànKàn, TĀ ShìbÚShì Zuì Piàoliang*de*. yǒuYĪTIĀN, nǚwánG Shàngwǎng Kàn SheiZuiPiaoLiangDe.com de*shÍHòu, TĀ Jiù Bù GĀOXìng le*. TĀ Bù GĀOXìng, YĪNWèi SheiZuiPiaoLiangDe.com SHUŌ, TĀ bÚShì Zuì Piàoliang*de*. SheiZuiPiaoLiangDe.com SHUŌ, Panda White Shì Zuì Piàoliang* de*.

　　女王 很 生气！ 她 跟 她的 朋友 说：
「我 很 生气！ 他们 说 我 不是 最漂亮的！
他们 说 Panda White 比 我 漂亮！ 不可思议！
Panda White 是 谁？ 」
　　女王 的 朋友 跟 她说： 「Panda White 是
很 漂亮的 熊猫。 」 女王 生气地 看了看 她。
　　「可是...可是， 她 不 比你 漂亮。」

Nǚwáng hěn shēngqì! Tā shēngqìde gēn tāpéngyǒu shuō: "Wǒ hěn shēngqì! tāmen shuō wǒ búshì zuì piàoliangde! Tāmen shuō Panda White bǐ wǒ piàoliang! bùkěsīyì! Panda White shi shéi?" Nǚwáng de péngyǒu gēntā shuō: "Panda White shì hěn piàoliangde xióngmāo."

Nǚwáng shēngqìde kànlekàn tā. "Kěshì...kěshì, tā bù bǐ nǐ piàoliang."

nǚwánG hěn SHĒNGQì! TĀ SHĒNGQìde* GĒN TĀpénGyǒu SHUŌ: "wǒ hěn SHĒNGQì! TĀmen* SHUŌ wǒ bÚShì Zuì Piàoliang*de*! TĀmen SHUŌ Panda White bǐ wǒ Piàoliang*! BùkěSĪYì! Panda White shi shéI?"

nǚwánG de* pénGyǒu GĒNTĀ SHUŌ: "Panda White Shì hěn Piàoliang*de* xiónGMĀO." nǚwánG SHĒNGQìde* Kànle*Kàn TĀ. "kěShì...kěShì, TĀ Bù bǐ nǐ Piàoliang*."

因为 女王 很 生气， 所以 她 跟 她的 朋友 说：
「SheiZuiPiaoLiangDe.com 说， Panda White 比我 漂亮！
我 要 Panda White 去 动物园！ 」

女王 的 朋友 说： 「去 动物园 吗？ 可是 在 动物园
的 动物 不可以 上网！ 动物园 不好！ 」

女王 说： 「就是。 因为 动物园 的 动物 不上
SheiZuiPiaoLiangDe.com ！ 所以 我 就 是 最 漂亮的了！ 」

Yīnwèi nǔwáng hěn shēngqì, suǒyǐ tā gēn tāde péngyǒu shuō: "SheiZuiPiaoliangDe.com shuō, Panda White bǐ wǒ piàoliang! Panda White yào qù dòngwùyuán!"

Nǔwáng de péngyǒu shuō: "Qù dòngwùyuán ma? Kěshì zài dòngwùyuán dòngwù bùkěyǐ shàngwǎng! Dòngwùyuán bùhǎo!"

Nǔwáng shuō: "Jiùshì. Yīnwèi dòngwùyuán de dòngwù bú shàng sheizuipiaoliang.com, suǒyǐ wǒ jiù shì zuì piàoliangde le!"

YĪNWèi nǔwánG hěn SHĒNGQì, suǒyǐ TĀ GĒN TĀde* pénGyǒu SHUŌ: "SheiZuiPiaoliangDe.com SHUŌ, Panda White bǐ wǒ Piàoliang*! wǒ Yào Panda White Qù DòngWùyuáN!"

nǔwánG de* pénGyǒu SHUŌ: "Qù DòngWùyuáN ma*? kěShì Zài DòngWùyuáN de* DòngWù Bùkěyǐ Shàngwǎng! DòngWùyuáN Bùhǎo!"

nǔwánG SHUŌ: "Jiù Shì. YĪNWèi DòngWùyuáN de* DòngWù bÚ Shàng SheiZuiPiaoLiangDe.com, suǒyǐ wǒ Jiù Shì Zuì Piàoliang*de* le*!"

女王 的 朋友 去 Panda White 的家。

「你好！ 我们 去 动物园， 好不好？」

「请问， 你 是 谁？」

「我 是 女王 的 朋友。 女王 要 你 去 动物园。」

「可是， 我 不 喜欢 动物园。」

「你 不喜欢 动物园 吗？ 不可思议！ 动物园 比你 的 家 好。 动物园 很 好！ 我们 去 看看, 好不好?」

Nǚwáng de péngyǒu qù Panda White de jiā. "Nǐ hǎo! Wǒmen qù dòngwùyuán, hǎobùhǎo?"

"Qǐngwèn, nǐ shì shéi?"

"Wǒ shì nǚwáng de péngyǒu. Nǚwáng yào nǐ qù dòngwùyuán."

"Kěshì, wǒ bù xǐhuān dòngwùyuán."

"Nǐ bù xǐhuān dòngwùyuán ma? Bùkěsīyì! Dòngwùyuán bǐ nǐde jiā hǎo. Dòngwùyuán hěn hǎo! Wǒmen qù kànkan, hǎobùhǎo?"

nǚwánG de* pénGyǒu Qù Panda White de* JIĀ. "nǐ hǎo! wǒmen* Qù DòngWùyuáN, hǎoBùhǎo?"

"qǐngWèn, nǐ Shì shéI?"

"wǒ Shì nǚwánG de* pénGyǒu. nǚwánG Yào nǐ Qù DòngWùyuáN."

"kěShì, wǒ Bù xǐHUĀN DòngWùyuáN."

"nǐ Bù xǐHUĀN DòngWùyuáN ma*? BùkěSĪYì! DòngWùyuáN bǐ nǐde* JIĀ hǎo. DòngWùyuáN hěn hǎo! wǒmen* Qù Kànkan*, hǎoBùhǎo?"

在 动物园， Panda White 说：「你看，
有 臭鼬 帽子， 是 黑白的！ 你把 一顶
臭鼬 帽子 给 女王， 跟她说 我 死了，
好不好？」

Panda White 给 她 四毛九。

女王的 朋友 就 买了 一顶 臭鼬 帽子。

Zài dòngwùyuán, Panda White shuō: "Nǐ kàn, yǒu chòuyòu màozǐ, shì hēibái de! Nǐ bǎ yīdǐng chòuyòu màozǐ gěi nǚwáng, gēntā shuō wǒ sǐle, hǎobùhǎo?"

Panda White gěi tā sìmáojiǔ. Nǚwángde péngyǒu jiù mǎile yīdǐng chòuyòu màozǐ.

Zài DòngWùyuáN, Panda White SHUŌ: "nǐ Kàn, yǒu ChòuYòu Màozǐ, Shì HĒIbáI de*! nǐ bǎ YĪdǐng ChòuYòu Màozǐ gěi nǚwánG, GĒNTĀ SHUŌ wǒ sǐle*, hǎoBùhǎo?"

Panda White gěi TĀ SìmáOjǐu. nǚwánGde* pénGyǒu Jìu mǎile* YĪdǐng ChòuYòu Màozǐ.

女王的 朋友 把 她买的 臭鼬 帽子 给了女王。

女王 很 高兴。「这顶 帽子 是 黑白的。 熊猫 也是 黑白 的。Panda White 死了！我 是 最 漂亮的 了！」

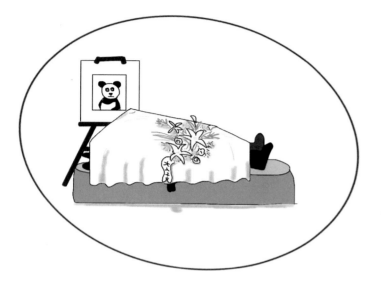

Nǔwángde péngyǒu bǎ tāmǎide chòuyòu màozǐ gěile nǔwáng. Nǔwáng hěn gāoxìng. "Zhèdǐng màozǐ shì hēibáide. Xióngmāo yěshì hēibáide. Panda White sǐ le! Wǒ shì zuì piàoliangde le!"

nǔwánGde* pénGyǒu bǎ TĀmǎide* ChòuYòu Màozǐ gěile* nǔwánG.

nǔwánG hěn GĀOXìng. "Zhèdǐng Màozǐ Shì HĒIbáIde*. xiónGMĀO yěShì HĒIbáIde*. Panda White sǐ le*! wǒ Shì Zuì Piàoliang*de* le*!"

可是 Panda White 没有 死。 她 在
动物园， 可是 她 没有 死。
　她 高兴， 因为 她 没有 死。
　可是， 她 很 想 吃 竹子。

Kěshì Panda White méiyǒu sǐ. Tā zài dòngwùyuán, kěshì tā méiyǒu sǐ. Tā gāoxìng, yīnwèi tā méiyǒu sǐ. Kěshì, tā hěn xiǎng chī zhúzi.

kěShì Panda White méIyǒu sǐ. TĀ Zài DòngWùyuáN, kěShì TĀ méIyǒu sǐ. TĀ GĀOXìng, YĪNWèi TĀ méIyǒu sǐ.

kěShì, TĀ hěn xiǎng CHĪ zhÚzi*.

Pandarella 跟 Pad Britt 在 动物园。

Panda White 问 Pandarella：「请问，动物园 有 竹子 吗？」

「没有。 可是 动物园 的 水饺 很好吃！」

Panda White 问 Pandarella：「请问 水饺 在 哪儿？」

Pandarella 跟她说 水饺 在 哪儿。

Pandarella gēn Pad Britt zài dòngwùyuan. Panda White wèn Pandarella: "Qǐngwèn, dòngwùyuán yǒu zhúzi ma?"

"Méiyǒu. Kěshì dòngwùyuán de shuǐjiǎo hěn hǎochī!"

Panda White wèn Pandarella: "Qǐngwèn shuǐjiǎo zài nǎr?"

Pandarella gēntā shuō shuǐjiǎo zài nǎr.

Pandarella GĒN Pad Britt Zài DòngWùyuáN. Panda White Wèn Pandarella: "qǐngWèn, DòngWùyuáN yǒu zhÚzi* ma*?"

"méIyǒu. kěShì DòngWùyuáN de* shuǐjiǎo hěn hǎoCHĪ!"

Panda White Wèn Pandarella: "qǐngWèn shuǐjiǎo Zài nǎr?"

Pandarella GĒNTĀ SHUŌ shuǐjiǎo Zài nǎr.

Panda White 去 水饺 饭馆。在 饭馆 人 很多。他们 都想吃 水饺，可是 没有 了。

在 饭馆 有 七个 小 动物。他们 都 在 睡觉。

Panda White 说：「没有 水饺 了！请问，你们 为什麼在 水饺 饭馆 睡觉？」

一个 小 动物 跟她说：「因为 我们 是 树懒。」

Panda White 说：「可是，你们 树懒 都 睡觉。饭馆的 水饺 是 谁 包的？」

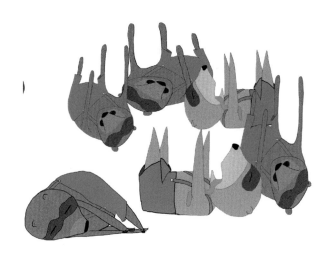

Panda White qù shuǐjiǎo fànguǎn. Zài fànguǎn, rén hěnduō. Tāmen dōu xiǎng chī shuijiǎo, kěshì méiyǒu le.

Zài fànguǎn yǒu qīge xiǎo dòngwù. Tāmen dōu zài shuìjiào. Panda White shuō: "Méiyou shuǐjiǎo le! qǐngwèn, nǐmen wèishénme zài shuǐjiǎo fànguǎn shuìjiào?"

Yīge xiǎo dòngwù gēntā shuō: "Yīnwèi wǒmen shì shùlǎn."

Panda White shuō: "Kěshì, nǐmen shùlǎn dōu zài shuìjiào. fànguǎn de shuǐjiǎo shì shéi bāode?"

Panda White Qù shuǐjiǎo Fànguǎn. Zài Fànguǎn réN hěnDUŌ. TĀmen* DŌU xiǎng CHĪ shuǐjiǎo, kěShì méIyǒu le*.

Zài Fànguǎn yǒu QĪge* xiǎo DòngWù. TĀmen* DŌU Zài ShuìJiào. Panda White SHUŌ: "méIyou shuǐjiǎo le*! qǐngWèn, nǐmen* WèishéNme* Zài shuǐjiǎo Fànguǎn ShuìJiào?" YĪge* xiǎo DòngWù GĒNTĀ SHUŌ: "YĪNWèi wǒmen* Shì Shùlǎn."

Panda White SHUŌ: "kěShì, nǐmen* Shùlǎn DŌU Zài ShuìJiào. Fànguǎn de* shuǐjiǎo Shì shéI BĀOde*?"

可是 七个 树懒 都 睡觉 了。

因为 树懒 都 睡觉, 虽然 要 买 水饺 的人 很多, 可是 没有 水饺 了。

所以 Panda White 就 包了 很多 水饺。

Kěshì qīge shùlǎn dōu shuìjiào le. Yīnwèi shùlǎn dōu shuìjiào, suīrán yào mǎi shuǐjiǎo derén hěnduō, kěshì dōu méiyǒu shuǐjiǎo le.

Suǒyǐ Panda White jiù bāole hěnduō shuǐjiǎo.

kěShì QĪge* Shùlǎn DŌU ShuìJiào le*. YĪNWèi Shùlǎn DŌU ShuìJiào, SUĪráN Yào mǎi shuǐjiǎo de*réN hěnDUŌ, kěShì méIyǒu shuǐjiǎo le*.

suǒyǐ Panda White Jiù BĀOle* hěnDUŌ shuǐjiǎo.

Panda White 包的 水饺 都 很好 吃，所以 很多 人 都 买了。

可是 因为 很多 人 都 买了 水饺，饭馆 没有 猪肉 了。

Panda White bāode shuǐjiǎo dōu hěn hǎochī, suǒyǐ hěnduō rén dōu mǎi le.

Kěshì yīnwèi hěnduō rén dōu mǎile shuǐjiǎo, fànguǎn méiyǒu zhūròu le.

Panda White BĀOde* shuǐjiǎo DŌU hěn hǎoCHĪ, suǒyǐ hěnDUŌ réN DŌU mǎi le*.

kěShì YĪNWèi hěnDUŌ réN DŌU mǎile* shuǐjiǎo, Fànguǎn méIyǒu ZHŪRòu le*.

Panda White 跟 七个 树懒 说:「不要
睡觉 了！ 不要 睡觉 了！ 猪肉
没有 了！」
所以 七个 树懒 就 去 J-Mart 买 猪肉。

Panda White gēn qīge shùlǎn shuō: "Búyào shuìjiào le! Búyào shuìjiào le! Zhūròu méiyǒu le!"
Suǒyǐ qīge shùlǎn jiù qù J-Mart mǎi zhūròu.

Panda White GĒN QĪge* Shùlǎn SHUŌ: "bÚYào ShuìJiào le*! bÚYào ShuìJiào le*! ZHŪRòu méIyǒu le*!"

suǒyǐ QĪge* Shùlǎn Jiù Qù J-Mart mǎi ZHŪRòu.

树懒 不在 饭馆 的时候，女王 就 来了。
女王 不是 来 饭馆 吃 水饺 的。 她 也
不是 来 饭馆 包 水饺 的。 她 来 饭馆，
因为 她 要 Panda White 吃 很多 年糕！

Shùlǎn búzài fànguǎn deshíhòu, nǔwáng jiù láile.

Nǚwáng búshì lái fànguǎn chī shuǐjiǎo de. Tā yě búshì lái fànguǎn bāo shuǐjiǎo de. Tā lái fànguǎn, yīnwèi tā yào Panda White chī hěnduō niángāo!

Shùlǎn bÚZài Fànguǎn de*shÍHòu, nǔwánG Jìu láIle*.

nǔwánG bÚShì láI Fànguǎn CHĪ shuǐjiǎo de*. TĀ yě bÚShì láI Fànguǎn BĀO shuǐjiǎo de*. TĀ láI Fànguǎn, YĪNWèi TĀ Yào Panda White CHĪ hěnDUŌ niáNGĀO!

可是 因为 Panda White 吃了 很多 年糕，
她 就 睡觉 了。 她 在 饭馆 睡觉。

七个 树懒 看到 了 Panda White 的 时候，
他们 都 不 高兴。

「猪肉 买好 了 ！ 请问， 你 为什麼 睡觉？

「她 睡觉 了 ！ 不要 睡觉 吧 ！」

Kěshì yīnwèi Panda White chīle hěnduō niángāo, tā jiù shuìjiào le. Tā zài fànguǎn lǐmiàn shuìjiào.

Qīge shùlǎn kàndàole Panda White de shíhòu, tāmen dōu bù gāoxìng. "Zhūròu mǎihǎole! qǐngwèn, nǐ wèishénme shuìjiào?"

"nǐ shuìjiào le! búyào shuìjiào ba!"

kěShì YĪNWèi Panda White CHĪle* hěnDUŌ niáNGĀO, TĀ Jìu ShuìJiào le*. TĀ Zài Fànguǎn ShuìJiào. QĪge* Shùlǎn KànDàole*Panda White de* shíHòu, TĀmen* DŌU Bù GĀOXìng.

"ZHŪRòu mǎihǎole*! qǐngWèn, nǐ WèishéNme* ShuìJiào?"

"TĀ ShuìJiào le*! bÚYào ShuìJiào ba*!"

我很想睡觉

　　一个 树懒 说： 「我们 去 四毛九 的 家。 他 唱 饶舌音乐， 所以 他的 家 会 很吵。」

　　「对！ 饶舌音乐 会 吵得 Panda White 不会 睡觉 了！」

　　所以 六个 树懒 都 去 四毛九 的 家。

　　（一个 树懒 不喜欢 饶舌音乐， 所以 他 在 饭馆 包水饺。）

Yīge shùlǎn shuō: "Wǒmen qù sìmáojiǔ de jiā. Tā chàng ráoshé yīnyuè, suǒyǐ tāde jiā huì hěn chǎo."

"Duì! Ráoshé yīnyuè chǎode Panda White búhuì shuìjiào le!"

Suǒyǐ liùge shùlǎn dōu qù sìmáojiǔ de jiā. (Yīge shùlǎn bù xǐhuān raoshé yīnyuè, suǒyǐ tā zài fànguǎn bāo shuǐjiǎo.)

Yīge* Shùlǎn SHUŌ: "wǒmen Qù SìmáOjǐu de* JIĀ. TĀ Chàng ráOshÉ YĪNYuè, suǒyǐ TĀde* JIĀ Huì hěn chǎo."

"Duì! ráOshÉ YĪNYuè chǎode* Panda White bÚHuì ShuìJiào le*!"

suǒyǐ Lìuge* Shùlǎn DŌU Qù SìmáOjǐu de* JIĀ. (YĪge* Shùlǎn Bù xǐHUĀN ráOshE YĪNYuè, suǒyǐ TĀ Zài Fànguǎn BĀO shuǐjiǎo.)

四毛九 的家 很吵。 四毛九 的家 吵得
六个 树懒 很 不 高兴。他的 家 比 有
五十三个 人 的 中文课 吵, 因为 四毛九 的
饶舌音乐 很吵！

可是 因为 树懒 不要 Panda White 睡觉,
所以 他们 去 四毛九 的家。

Sìmáojiǔ de jiā hěn chǎo. Sìmáojiǔ de jiā chǎode* liùge shùlǎn hěn bù gāoxìng. Tāde jiā bǐ yǒu wǔshísānge rén de zhōngwénkè chǎo, yīnwèi sìmáojiǔ de ráoshé yīnyuè hěn chǎo! Kěshì yīnwèi tāmen búyào Panda White shuìjiào le, suǒyǐ tāmen qù sìmáojiǔ de jiā.

SìmáOjǐu de* JIĀ hěn chǎo. SìmáOjǐu de* JIĀ chǎode* Lìuge* Shùlǎn hěn Bù GĀOXìng. TĀ de* JIĀ bǐ yǒu wǔshÍSĀNge* réN de* ZHŌNGwéNKè chǎo, YĪNWèi SìmáOjǐu de* ráOshÉ YĪNYuè hěn chǎo! kěShì YĪNWèi Shùlǎn bÚYào Panda White ShuìJiào le*, suǒyǐ TĀmen* Qù SìmáOjǐu de* JIĀ.

Panda White

不 睡 觉 了 ！

Panda White
bú shuìjiào le!

Panda White
bÚ ShuìJiào le*!

Panda White 跟 四毛九 说：「请问，这 是 什麼 音乐？」

四毛九 跟她说：「这 是 饶舌音乐。你 喜欢 吗？」

Panda White gēn sìmáojiǔ shuō: "Qǐngwèn, zhè shì shénme yīnyuè?"

Sìmáojiǔ gēntā shuō: "Zhè shì ráoshé yīnyuè. Nǐ xǐhuān ma?"

Panda White GĒN SìmáOjǐu SHUŌ: "qǐngWèn, Zhè Shì shéNme* YĪNYuè?"

SìmáOjǐu GĒNTĀ SHUŌ: "Zhè Shì ráOshÉ YĪNYuè. nǐ xǐHUĀN ma*?"

Panda White 很 喜欢！她 跟 四毛九 说：
「我 跟你 唱 饶舌音乐，好吗？」
四毛九 说：「不可思议！」
可是 因为 Panda White 唱 饶舌音乐
唱得 很 好，所以 她 跟 四毛九 就 去
Hollywood 唱 饶舌音乐。

Panda White hěn xǐhuān! Tā gēn sìmáojiǔ shuō: "Wǒ gēn nǐ chàng ráoshé yīnyuè, hǎo ma?"

Sìmáojiǔ shuō: "Bùkěsīyì!"

Kěshì yīnwèi Panda White chàng ráoshé yīnyuè chàngde* hěn hǎo, suǒyǐ tā gēn sìmáojiǔ jiù qù Hollywood chàng ráoshè yīnyuè.

Panda White hěn xǐHUĀN! TĀ GĒN SìmáOjǐu SHUŌ: "wǒ GĒN nǐ Chàng ráOshÉ YĪNYuè, hǎo ma*?"

SìmáOjǐu SHUŌ: "BùkěSĪYì!"

kěShì YĪNWèi Panda White Chàng ráOshÉ YĪNYuè Chàngde* hěn hǎo, suǒyǐ TĀ GĒN SìmáOjǐu Jiù Qù Hollywood Chàng ráOShè YĪNYuè.

　女王 很 生气！她 很 生气, 因为 Panda White 有 钱 了. 女王 很 生气, 因为 她 买 了 很 多 年糕, 所以 她 没 有 钱 了。
　因为 她 没 有 钱 了, 所以 她 就 要 在 J-Mart 卖 Panda White 的 T恤 了。

nǔwánG hěn SHĒNGQì! TĀ hěn SHĒNGQì, YĪNWèi Panda White yǒu qiáN le*. nǔwánG hěn SHĒNGQì, YĪNWèi TĀ mǎile* hěnDUŌ niáNGĀO, suǒyǐ TĀ méIyǒu qiáN le*. YĪNWèi TĀ méIyǒu qiáN le*, suǒyǐ TĀ Yào Zài J-Mart Mài Panda White de* T-xù le*.

Nǔwáng hěn shēngqì! Tā hěn shēngqì, yīnwèi Panda White yǒu qián le. Nǔwáng hěn shēngqì, yīnwèi tā mǎile hěnduō niángāo, suǒyǐ tā méiyǒu qián le. Yīnwèi tā méiyǒu qián le, suǒyǐ tā yào zài J-Mart mài Panda White de T-xù le.

bǎ 把 : grab-it-and…
ba 吧 : let's…
bāo 包 : wrap, hug
bāo shuǐjiǎo 包水饺 : wrap dumplings
bǐ 比 : compared to
bú, bù 不 : not
búyào 不要 : don't! doesn't want to
bùkěsīyì 不可思议 : inconceivable!
bùkěyǐ 不可以 : not allowed to
chàng 唱 : sing
chàngde 唱得 : sings in a way that is…
chǎo 吵 : is noisy
chǎode 吵得 : is so noisy that…
chī 吃 : eats
chòuyòu 臭鼬 : skunk

cóngqián 从前 : Once upon a time…
dàjiā 大家 : everyone
de 的 : the one that…
dejiā 的家 : 's home
derén 的人 : a person that…
deshíhòu 的时候 : at the time when…
dòngwù 动物 : animal
dòngwùyuán 动物园 : zoo
dōu 都 : all
duì 对 : is correct; that's right!
fànguǎn 饭馆 : restaurant
fěnhóngsè de 粉红色的 : pink
gāoxìng 高兴 : is/are happy
gěi 给 : gives
gēn 跟 : with
gēntāshuō 跟她说 : says to her
hǎo 好 : is good
hǎobùhǎo 好不好 : okay?
hǎoma 好吗 : okay?

hémǎ 河马 : hippopotamus
hēibái 黑白 : black and white
hēibái de 黑白的 : black and white
hěn 很 : very
hěnduō 很多 : numerous many
hěnhǎochī 很好吃 : delicious
hóngsè de 红色的 : red
huì 会 : is likely to
jiā 家 : home
jiù 就 : sooner-than-expected, easier-than-expected
jiùshì 就是 : that's just it!
kàn 看 : look, read
kànkàn 看看 : glance at
kànlekàn 看了看 : glanced at
kěshì 可是 : but
kǒuhóng 口红 : lipstick
lái 来 : come
le 了 : (shows completed action)

liùge 六个：six
ma 吗：yes-or-no?
mǎi 买：buys
mǎide 买的：the ones that someone bought
mǎihǎole 买好了：all bought! Finished shopping
mài 卖：sells
màozi 帽子：hat
méiyǒu 没有：doesn't have, there isn't
měiguó xiǎojiě 美国小姐：Miss America
nǎr 哪儿：where?
nàr 那儿：there
nǐ 你：you
nǐ hǎo 你好：hello
nǐ kàn 你看：look!
nǐde 你的：your
nǐmen 你们：y'all
niángāo 年糕："New Year's Cake" made of sticky rice
nǚrén 女人：woman
nǚwáng 女王：queen ("female king")
péngyǒu 朋友：friend
piàoliàngde 漂亮的：the pretty one
piàoliang 漂亮：pretty
qīge 七个：seven
qián 钱：money
qǐngwèn 请问：excuse me…
qù 去：goes
ráoshé yīnyuè 饶舌音乐：rap music
rén 人：person
shàngwǎng 上网：goes online
shéi 谁：who?
shénme 什麼：what?
shēngqì 生气：is angry
shēngqì de 生气地：angrily
shì 是：is, are, am, be, was, were
shìbúshì 是不是：is it?
shùlǎn 树懒：sloth
shuǐjiǎo 水饺：boiled dumplings
shuìjiào 睡觉：sleep
shuō 说：says
sǐ 死：dies
sǐle 死了：is dead

sìmáijiǔ 四毛九：49 cents
suīrán 虽然：although
suǒyǐ 所以：therefore
t xù t恤：T-shirt
tā 她：she
tā 他：he
tā mǎide 他买的：the one that he buys
tāde 他的：his
tāde 她的：her
tāmen 他们：they
wèishénme 为什麼：why?
wèn 问：asks
wǒ 我：I me
wǒmen 我们：we us
wǔshísān ge 五十三个：53
xǐhuān 喜欢：likes
xiǎng 想：feels like
xiǎngchī 想吃：feels like eating
xiǎo 小：is small
xióngmāo 熊猫：panda
yào 要：must
yě 也：also
yīdǐng 一顶：one, a (referring to a hat)
yìge 一个：one
yīnwèi 因为：because
yīnyuè 音乐：music
yǒu 有：there is has
yǒude 有的：some
yǒuyītiān 有一天：one day…
zài 在：be at a place
zhè 这：this
zhèdǐng 这顶：this (referring to a hat)
zhèzhī 这只：this
zhōngwénkè 中文课：Chinese class
zhūròu 猪肉：pork
zhúzǐ 竹子：bamboo
zuì 最：the most
zuì piàoliàng 最漂亮：the prettiest

Made in the USA
Middletown, DE
15 July 2017